BELL BOTTOM

MR VIVEK KUMAR PANDEY SHAMBHUNATH

ISBN 979-888546523-6

During writing this book no character & no religious are harmed written by Mr Vivek Kumar Pandey. Winner Youngest Writer Award 1st Rank In India 2020.He Is Only One Writer Can Publish 700+ Own Book That Was Greatest Successfull In His Life. This All Credit Goes To My Super Hero Daddy. In This Book Deeply Given About Hijacking Of Indian Aeroplane.Totally Bell Bottom Film Based On This Real Story Of Hijacking Of Planes.

Contents

Foreword   *vii*

  1. Khalistan Movement (bell Bottom)   1

Indian Airlines Flight 423

  2. List Of Hijackings Of Indian Aeroplanes   25

  3. Bell Bottom (2021 Film)   30

Foreword

Author biography in English :MY NAME IS VIVEK KUMAR PANDEY . I WAS BORN IN 30 SEP 2002,I AM FROM SURAT GUJARAT INDIA.MY DREAM WAS TO BE GOOD WRITERS ,MY FAMILY SUPPORTED ME TO SUCCESSFUL AND I CAN DO IT MY SELF.How do I write? That is a question, I believe, that can be honestly answered by me."CELEBRATING YOUNGEST WRITER AWARD WINNER IN GUJARAT 1ST RANK" MR PANDEY JI . I may think I did a good job writing something when in reality it could be horrible. The reader is the one who decides the quality of my writing. I do find writing to be natural to me and therefore find it to be a real challenge. My trick as a challenged writer is to do the best I can and know that I am happy with the final outcome. It may take a while to do my best and there may be quite a few problems I run into along the way.

I am not a greedy person those who are thinking about me and my self I never tried it anyone people suffering from sadness ,I trying to get promoted people suffering from happiness and joy in your Life Time. Now in current situation in India and also world people are unemployed and have no many but our indian governor help to people to get free food from ration card , i also take part in leadership team ,i am Motivational speaker , Film script writer. There was my two dream firstly writer and secondly actor & also my own film is upcoming soon i done almost completely completed script for my film .I AM GOING TO SAY WORD OF HEART TOUCH OUT PLEASE READ IT" , firstly i thanks my father he supports me in this field they always getting inspired me by own his words and behavior ,they always said that he was a biggest person in the world in future and also they purchase fruit and chocolate for me in anytime & anyway , firstly my father buy him then call me Vivek you want a chocolate i will say yes papa but how many tell me ,papa: you tell me how much i buy him i told 1 or 2 chocolate but my father purchase whole the boxes of chocolate and they get suprised me. MY FATHER WAS BORN IN " 20 SEPTEMBER" 1971 IN INDIA.

1) MY FATHER FAVORITE CLOTHES IS KURTA PAIJMA AND ALSO STYLES SHOE

2) FAVORITE SINGER IS KISHORE DA

3) FAVORITE STATE GUJARAT AND KOLKATA , HIS VILLAGE IN BIHAR

4) FAVORITE COLOR BLACK AND WHITE

THEY ALSO LOVE cricket like IPL and one day t-20 .they also like watching a News daily and heard the song daily ,they also interested in tik tok video but in current time tik tok is banned in india but also few videos are in you tube. In lockdown time my family and me very enjoy day daily. my father play daily ludo with his sister and son, daughter.they always loved tea and coffee anytime call me "। वविेक थोडा़ चाय बनाओना वविेक तम्ुहारे हाथ का चाय अच्छा लगता है". I make it tea for my father but some reason after the April to june they are suffering from fever and cough , weakness on 6 June 2020 my father death. they not told me say bye bye his life. After death of 6 June on 10 june my mom and dad anniversary.but my father is Best in the world they can do anything for me please take care of father and respect it of your parents.

Khalistan movement (Bell Bottom)

- *Khalistan movement (Bell Bottom)*

1. *In This Book Deeply Given About Hijacking Of Indian Aeroplane.Totally Bell Bottom Film Based On This Real Story Of Hijacking Of Planes.*

Flag of Khalistan

The Khalistan movement is a Sikh separatist movement seeking to create a homeland for Sikhs by establishing a sovereign state, called Khālistān ('Land of the Khalsa'), in the Punjab region. The proposed state would consist of land that currently forms Punjab, India and Punjab, Pakistan.

Ever since the separatist movement gathered force in the 1980s, the territorial ambitions of Khalistan have at times included Chandigarh, sections of the Indian Punjab, including the whole of North India, and some parts of the western states of India. Prime Minister of Pakistan Zulfikar Ali Bhutto, according to Jagjit Singh Chohan, had proposed all out help to create Khalistan during his talks with Chohan, following the conclusion of the Indo-Pakistani War of 1971.

- The call for a separate Sikh state began in the wake of the fall of the British Empire. In 1940, the first explicit call for Khalistan was made in a pamphlet titled "Khalistan". With financial and political support of the Sikh diaspora, the movement flourished in the Indian state of Punjab – which has a Sikh-majority population – continuing through the 1970s and 1980s, and reaching its zenith in the late 1980s. In the 1990s, the insurgency petered out, and the movement failed to reach its objective for multiple reasons including a heavy police crackdown on separatists, factional infighting, and disillusionment from the Sikh population.

There is some support within India and the Sikh diaspora, with yearly demonstrations in protest of those killed during Operation Blue Star. In early 2018, some militant groups were arrested by police in Punjab, India. Chief Minister of Punjab Amarinder Singh claimed that the recent extremism is backed by Pakistan's Inter-Services Intelligence (ISI) and "Khalistani sympathisers" in Canada, Italy, and the UK.

- Maharaja Ranjit Singh's Sikh Empire at its peak in c. 1839 most of which is currently under Pakistan

Sikhs have been concentrated in the Punjab region of South Asia. Before its conquest by the British, the region around Punjab had been ruled by the confederacy of Sikh Misls founded by Banda Bahadur. The Misls ruled over the entire Punjab from 1767 to 1799, until their confederacy was unified into the Sikh Empire by Maharajah Ranjit Singh from 1799 to 1849.

At the end of the Second Anglo-Sikh War in 1849, the Sikh Empire dissolved into separate princely states and the British province of Punjab.As a result of the British 'divide and conquer' process, which involved differentiating and designating religions into communal boundaries, many religious nationalist movement emerged among the Hindus, Buddhists, Muslims, and the Sikhs. .

As the British Empire began to dissolve in the 1930s, Sikhs made their first call for a Sikh homeland. When the Lahore Resolution of the Muslim League demanded Punjab be made into a Muslim state, the Akalis viewed it as an attempt to usurp a historically Sikh territory. In response, the Sikh party Shiromani Akali Dal argued for a community that was separate from Hindus and Muslims. The Akali Dal imagined Khalistan as a theocratic state led by the Maharaja of Patiala with the aid of a cabinet consisting of the representatives of other units.The country would include parts of present-day Punjab, India, present-day Punjab, Pakistan (including Lahore), and the Simla Hill States.

- *Partition of India, 1947*

British Punjab Province, in 1909

Before the 1947 partition of India, Sikhs were not in majority in any of the districts of pre-partition British Punjab Province other than Ludhiana (where Sikhs formed 41.6% of the population). Rather, districts in the region had a majority of either the Hindus or Muslims depending on its location in the province.

British India was partitioned on a religious basis in 1947, where the Punjab province was divided between India and the newly-created Pakistan. As result, a majority of Sikhs, along with the Hindus, migrated from the Pakistani region to India's Punjab, which included present-day Haryana and Himachal Pradesh. The Sikh population, which had gone as high as 19.8% in some Pakistani districts in 1941, dropped to 0.1% in Pakistan, and rose sharply in the districts assigned to India. However, they would still be a minority in the Punjab province of India, which remained a Hindu-majority province.

- *Sikh relationship with Punjab (via Oberoi)*

Map of the present-day Indian state of Punjab. Following the partition, East Punjab became PEPSU, which was further divided in 1966 with the formation of the new states of Haryana and Himachal Pradesh as well as the current state of Punjab. Punjab is the only state in India with a majority Sikh population.

Sikh historian Harjot Singh Oberoi argues that, despite the historical linkages between Sikhs and Punjab, territory has never been a major element of Sikh self-definition. He makes the case that the attachment of Punjab with Sikhism is a recent phenomenon, stemming from the 1940s. Historically, Sikhism has been pan-Indian, with the Guru Granth Sahib (the main scripture of Sikhism) drawing from works of saints in both North and South India, while several major seats in Sikhism (e.g. Nankana Sahib in Pakistan, Takht Sri Patna Sahib in Bihar, and Hazur Sahib in Maharashtra) are located outside of Punjab.

Oberoi makes the case that Sikh leaders in the late 1930s and 1940s realized that the dominance of Muslims in Pakistan and of Hindus in India was imminent. To justify a separate Sikh state within the Punjab, Sikh leaders started to mobilize meta-commentaries and signs to argue that Punjab belonged to Sikhs and Sikhs belong to Punjab. This began the territorialization of the Sikh community.

This territorialization of the Sikh community would be formalized in March 1946, when the Sikh political party of Akali Dal passed a resolution proclaiming the natural association of Punjab and the Sikh religious community. Oberoi argues that despite having its beginnings in the early 20th century, Khalistan as a separatist movement was never a major issue until the late 1970s and 1980s when it began to militarize.

- 1950s to 1970s

There are two distinct narratives about the origins of the calls for a sovereign Khalistan. One refers to the events within India itself, while the other privileges the role of the Sikh diaspora. Both of these narratives vary in the form of governance proposed for this state (e.g. theocracy vs democracy) as well as the proposed name (i.e. Sikhistan vs Khalistan). Even the precise geographical borders of the proposed state differs among them although it was generally imagined to be carved out from one of various historical constructions of the Punjab.

- Emergence in India

Established on 14 December 1920, Shiromani Akali Dal was a Sikh political party that sought to form a government in Punjab.

Following the 1947 independence of India, the Punjabi Suba movement, led by the Akali Dal, sought the creation of a province (suba) for Punjabi people. The Akali Dal's maximal position of demands was a sovereign state (i.e. Khalistan), while its minimal position was to have an autonomous state within India.The issues raised during the Punjabi Suba movement were later used as a premise for the creation of a separate Sikh country by proponents of Khalistan.

As the religious-based partition of India led to much bloodshed, the Indian government initially rejected the demand, concerned that creating a Punjabi-majority state would effectively mean yet again creating a state based on religious grounds.

However, in September 1966, the Union Government led by Indira Gandhi accepted the demand. On 7 September 1966, the Punjab Reorganisation Act was passed in Parliament, implemented with effect beginning 1 November 1966. Accordingly, Punjab was divided into the state of Punjab and Haryana, with certain areas to Himachal Pradesh. Chandigarh was made a centrally administered Union territory.

- Anandpur Resolution

As Punjab and Haryana now shared the capital of Chandigarh, resentment was felt among Sikhs in Punjab. Adding further grievance, a canal system was put in place over the rivers of Ravi, Beas, and Sutlej, which flowed through Punjab, in order for water to also reach Haryana and Rajasthan. As result, Punjab would only receive 23% of the water while the rest would go to the two other states. The fact that the issue would not be revisited brought on additional turmoil to Sikh resentment against Congress.

The Akali Dal was defeated in the 1972 Punjab elections. To regain public appeal, the party put forward the Anandpur Sahib Resolution in 1973 to demand radical devolution of power and further autonomy to Punjab. The resolution document included both religious and political issues, asking for the recognition of Sikhism as a religion separate from Hinduism, as well as the transfer of Chandigarh and certain other areas to Punjab. It also demanded that power be radically devolved from the central to state governments.

The document was largely forgotten for some time after its adoption until gaining attention in the following decade. In 1982, the Akali Dal and Jarnail Singh Bhindranwale joined hands to launch the Dharam Yudh Morcha in order to implement the resolution. Thousands of people joined the movement, feeling that it represented a real solution to such demands as larger shares of water for irrigation and the return of Chandigarh to Punjab.

- Emergence in the diaspora

According to the 'events outside India' narrative, particularly after 1971, the notion of a sovereign and independent state of Khalistan began to popularize among Sikhs in North America and Europe. One such account is provided by the Khalistan Council which had moorings in West London, where the Khalistan movement is said to have launched in 1970.

Davinder Singh Parmar migrated to London in 1954. According to Parmar, his first pro-Khalistan meeting was attended by less than 20 people and he was labelled as a madman, receiving only one person's support. Parmar continued his efforts despite the lack of a following, eventually raising the Khalistani flag in Birmingham in the 1970s. In 1969, two years after losing the Punjab Assembly elections, Indian politician Jagjit Singh Chohan moved to the United Kingdom to start his campaign for the creation of Khalistan. Apart from Punjab, Himachal, and Haryana, Chohan's proposal of Khalistan also included parts of Rajasthan state.

Parmar and Chohan would meet in 1970 and formally announce the Khalistan movement at a London press conference, though being largely dismissed by the community as fanatical fringe without any support.

- Chohan in Pakistan and US

Location of Nankana Sahib in Punjab, Pakistan, that was proposed as the capital of Khalistan by ZA Bhutto.

Following the Indo-Pakistani War of 1971, Chohan visited Pakistan as a guest of such leaders as Chaudhuri Zahoor Elahi. Visiting Nankana Sahib and several historical gurdwaras in Pakistan, Chohan utilized the opportunity to spread the notion of an independent Sikh state. Widely publicized by Pakistani press, the extensive coverage of his remarks introduced the international community, including those in India, to the demand of Khalistan for the first time. Though lacking public support, the term Khalistan became more and more recognizable. According to Chohan, during a talk with Prime Minister Zulfikar Ali Bhutto of Pakistan, Bhutto had proposed to make Nankana Sahib the capital of Khalistan.

On 13 October 1971, visiting the United States at the invitation of his supporters in the Sikh diaspora, Chohan placed an advertisement in the New York Times proclaiming an independent Sikh state. Such promotion enabled him to collect millions of dollars from the diaspora, eventually leading to charges in India relating to sedition and other crimes in connection with his separatist activities.

- Khalistan National Council

After returning to India in 1977, Chohan travelled to Britain in 1979. There, he would establish the Khalistan National Council, declaring its formation at Anandpur Sahib on 12 April 1980. Chohan designated himself as President of the Council and Balbir Singh Sandhu as its Secretary General.

In May 1980, Chohan travelled to London to announce the formation of Khalistan. A similar announcement was made in Amritsar by Sandhu, who released stamps and currency of Khalistan. Operating from a building termed "Khalistan House", Chohan named a Cabinet and declared himself president of the "Republic of Khalistan," issuing symbolic Khalistan 'passports,' 'postage stamps,' and 'Khalistan dollars.' Moreover, embassies in Britain and other European countries were opened by Chohan.[39] It is reported that, with the support of a wealthy Californian peach magnate, Chohan opened an Ecuadorian bank account to further support his operation. As well as maintaining contacts among various groups in Canada, the US, and Germany, Chohan kept in contact with the Sikh leader Jarnail Singh Bhindranwale who was campaigning for a theocratic Sikh homeland.

The globalized Sikh diaspora invested efforts and resources for Khalistan, but the Khalistan movement remained nearly invisible on the global political scene until the Operation Blue Star of June 1984.

- R&AW

In later disclosures from former R&AW special secretary G.B.S. Sidhu, R&AW itself helped "build the Khalistan legend," actively participated in the planning of Operation Blue Star. While posted in Ottawa, Canada in 1976 to look into the "Khalistan problem" among the Sikh diaspora, Sidhu found "nothing amiss" during the three years he was there, stating that "Delhi was unnecessarily making a mountain of a molehill where none existed," that the agency created seven posts in West Europe and North America in 1981 to counter non-existent Khalistan activities, and that the deployed officers were "not always familiar with the Sikhs or the Punjab issue." He described the secessionist movement as a "chimera" until the army operation, after which the insurgency would start.

According to a New York Times article written just a few weeks after the operation, "Before the raid on the Golden Temple, neither the Government nor anyone else appeared to put much credence in the Khalistan movement. Mr. Bhindranwale himself said many times that he was not seeking an independent country for Sikhs, merely greater autonomy for Punjab within the Indian Union....One possible explanation advanced for the Government's raising of the Khalistan question is that it needs to take every opportunity to justify the killing in Amritsar and the invasion of the Sikhs' holiest shrine."

Khushwant Singh had written that "considerable Khalistan sentiment seems to have arisen since the raid on the temple, which many Sikhs, if not most, have taken as a deep offense to their religion and their sensibilities," referring to the drastic change in community sentiments after the army attack.

- *Late 1970s to 1983*

- Delhi Asian Games (1982)

The Akali leaders, having planned to announce a victory for Dharam Yudh Morcha, were outraged by the changes to the agreed-upon settlement. In November 1982, Akali leader Harchand Singh Longowal announced that the party would disrupt the 9th annual Asian Games by sending groups of Akali workers to Delhi to intentionally get arrested. Following negotiations between the Akali Dal and the government failed at the last moment due to disagreements regarding the transfer of areas between Punjab and Haryana.

Knowing that the Games would receive extensive coverage, Akali leaders vowed to overwhelm Delhi with a flood of protestors, aiming to heighten the perception of Sikh "plight" among the international audience. A week before the Games, Bhajan Lal, Chief Minister of Haryana and member of the INC party, responded by sealing the Delhi-Punjab border, and ordering all Sikh visitors travelling from to Delhi from Punjab to be frisked. While such measures were seen as discriminatory and humiliating by Sikhs, they proved effective as Akali Dal could only organize small and scattered protests in Delhi. Consequently, many Sikhs who did not initially support Akalis and Bhindranwale began sympathizing with the Akali Morcha.

Following the conclusion of the Games, Longowal organised a convention of Sikh veterans at the Darbar Sahib. It was attended by a large number of Sikh ex-servicemen, including retd. Major General Shabeg Singh who subsequently became Bhindranwale's military advisor.

- 1984

Increasing militant activity
Widespread murders by followers of Bhindranwale occurred in 1980s' Punjab. Armed Khalistani militants of this period described themselves as kharku,most likely meaning 'noise maker,' from the Punjabi kharaka

('noise') in reference to their strident activity. In the period between 4 August 1982 and 3 June 1984, more than 1200 violent incidents took place, resulting in the death of 410 people and the injury of 1180.

On its own, the year 1984 (from 1 January to 3 June) saw 775 violent incidents, resulting in 298 people killed and 525 injured. One such murder was that of DIG Avtar Singh Atwal, killed on 25 April 1983 at the gate of the Darbar Sahib, whose corpse would remain at the place of death for 2 hours as even police officers were afraid to touch the body without Bhindranwale's permission. This showed the power and influence that Bhindranwale had over the region.

Though it was common knowledge that those responsible for such bombings and murders were taking shelter in gurdwaras, the INC Government of India declared that it could not enter these places of worship, for the fear of hurting Sikh sentiments. Even as detailed reports on the open shipping of arms-laden trucks were sent to Prime Minister Indira Gandhi, the Government would choose not to take action.Finally, following the murder of six Hindu bus passengers in October 1983, an emergency rule was imposed in Punjab, which would continue for more than a decade.

* Constitutional issues

The Akali Dal began more agitation in February 1984, protesting against Article 25, clause (2)(b), of the Indian Constitution, which ambiguously explains that "the reference to Hindus shall be construed as including a reference to persons professing the Sikh, Jaina, or Buddhist religion," while also implicitly recognizing Sikhism as a separate religion: "the wearing and carrying of kripans [sic] shall be deemed to be included in the profession of the Sikh religion."109 Even today, this clause is deemed offensive by many religious minorities in India due to its failure to recognise such religions separately under the constitution.

Members of the Akali Dal demanded that the removal of any ambiguity in the Constitution that refers to Sikhs as Hindu, as such prompts various concerns for the Sikh population, both in principle and in practice. For instance, a Sikh couple who would marry in accordance to the rites of their religion would have to register their union either under the Special Marriage Act, 1954 or the Hindu Marriage Act, 1955. The Akalis demanded replacement of such rules with laws specific to Sikhism.

- Operation Blue Star

The pro-Khalistan Sikh separatists within the Harmandir Sahib were led by former Major General Shabeg Singh

Operation Blue Star was an Indian military operation ordered by Prime Minister Indira Gandhi, between 1 and 8 June 1984, to remove militant religious leader Jarnail Singh Bhindranwale and his armed followers from the buildings of the Harmandir Sahib complex (aka the Golden Temple) in Amritsar, Punjab – the most sacred site in Sikhism.

In July 1983, Akali Dal President Harchand Singh Longowal had invited Bhindranwale to take up residence at the sacred temple complex, which the government would allege that Bhindranwale would later make into an armoury and headquarters for his armed uprising.

Since the inception of the Dharam Yudh Morcha to the violent events leading up to Operation Blue Star, Khalistani militants had directly killed 165 Hindus and Nirankaris, as well as 39 Sikhs opposed to Bhindranwale, while a total of 410 dead and 1,180 injured came as result of Khalistani violence and riots.

As negotiations held with Bhindranwale and his supporters proved unsuccessful, Indira Gandhi ordered the Indian Army to launch Operation Blue Star.Along with the Army, the operation would involve Central Reserve Police Force, Border Security Force, and Punjab Police. Army units led by Lt. Gen. Kuldip Singh Brar (a Sikh), surrounded the temple complex on 3 June 1984. Just before the commencement of the operation, Lt. Gen. Brar addressed the soldiers.

The action is not against the Sikhs or the Sikh religion; it is against terrorism. If there is anyone amongst them, who have strong religious sentiments or other reservations, and do not wish to take part in the operation he can opt out, and it will not be held against him.

- Lieutenant General Kuldip Singh Brar

However, none of the soldiers opted out, including many "Sikh officers, junior commissioned officers and other ranks."Using a public address system, the Army repeatedly demanded the militants to surrender, asking them to at least allow pilgrims to leave the temple premises before commencing battle.

Nothing happened until 7:00 PM (IST). The Army, equipped with tanks and heavy artillery, had grossly underestimated the firepower possessed by the militants, who attacked with anti-tank and machine-gun fire from the heavily fortified Akal Takht, and who possessed Chinese-made, rocket-propelled grenade launchers with armour-piercing capabilities. After a 24-hour shootout, the army finally wrested control of the temple complex.

Bhindranwale was killed in the operation, while many of his followers managed to escape. Army casualty figures counted 83 dead and 249 injured. According to the official estimate presented by the Indian Government, the event resulted in a combined total of 493 militant and civilian casualties, as well as the apprehension of 1592 individuals.

U.K. Foreign Secretary William Hague attributed high civilian casualties to the Indian Government's attempt at a full frontal assault on the militants, diverging from the recommendations provided by the U.K. Military. Opponents of Gandhi also criticised the operation for its excessive use of force. Lieutenant General Brar later stated that the Government had "no other recourse" due to a "complete breakdown" of the situation: state machinery was under the militants' control; declaration of Khalistan was imminent; and Pakistan would have come into the picture declaring its support for Khalistan.

* Indira Gandhi

On the morning of 31 October 1984, Indira Gandhi was assassinated in New Delhi by her two personal security guards Satwant Singh and Beant Singh, both Sikhs, in retaliation for Operation Blue Star. The assassination would trigger the 1984 Anti-Sikh Riots across North India. While the ruling party, Indian National Congress (INC), maintained that the violence was due to spontaneous riots, its critics have alleged that INC members themselves had planned a pogrom against the Sikhs.

The Nanavati Commission, a special commission created to investigate the riots, concluded that INC leaders (including Jagdish Tytler, H. K. L. Bhagat, and Sajjan Kumar) had directly or indirectly taken a role in the rioting incidents. Union Minister Kamal Nath was accused of leading riots near Rakab Ganj, but was cleared due to lack of evidence. Other political parties strongly condemned the riots. Two major civil-liberties organisations issued a joint report on the anti-Sikh riots, naming 16 significant politicians, 13 police officers, and 198 others, accused by survivors and eyewitnesses.

- 1985 Rajiv-Longowal Accord

This section needs additional citations for verification. Relevant discussion may be found on the talk page. Please help improve this article by adding citations to reliable sources. Unsourced material may be challenged and removed. (September 2019) (Learn how and when to remove this template message)

Many Sikh and Hindu groups, as well as organisations not affiliated to any religion, have attempted to establish peace between the Khalistan proponents and the Government of India. Akalis continued to witness radicalization of Sikh politics, fearing disastrous consequences. In response, President Harchand Singh Longowal reinstated the head of the Akali Dal and pushed for a peace initiative that reiterated the importance of Hindu-Sikh amity, condemning Sikh extremist violence, therefore declaring that the Akali Dal was not in favor of Khalistan.

In 1985, The Government of India attempted to seek a political solution to the grievances of the Sikhs through the Rajiv-Longowal Accord, which took place between Longowal and Prime Minister Rajiv Gandhi. The Accord – recognizing the religious, territorial, and economic demands of the Sikhs that were thought to be non-negotiable under Indira Gandhi's tenure – agreed to establish commissions and independent tribunals in order to resolve the Chandigarh issue and the river dispute, laying the basis for Akali Dal's victory in the coming elections.

Though providing a basis for a return to normality, Chandigarh evidently remained an issue and the agreement was denounced by Sikh militants who refused to give up the demand for an independent Khalistan. These extremists, who were left unappeased, would react by assassinating Longowal. Such behavior would lead to the dismissal of negotiations, whereby both Congress and the Akali parties accused each other of aiding terrorism.

The Indian Government pointed to the involvement of a "foreign hand," referring to Pakistan's abetting of the movement. Punjab noted to the Indian Government that militants were able to obtain sophisticated arms through sources outside the country and by developing links with sources within the country. As such, the Government believed that large illegal flows of arms were flowing through the borders of India, with Pakistan being responsible for trafficking arms. India claimed that Pakistan provided sanctuary, arms, money, and moral support to the militants, though most of the accusations were based on circumstantial evidence.

* Air India Flight 182

Irish Naval Service recovering bodies from the Air India Flight 182 bombing

The aircraft involved, VT-EFO, seen on 10 June 1985, less than two weeks before the bombing of Air India Flight 182

Air India Flight 182 was an Air India flight operating on the Montréal-London-Delhi-Bombay route. On 23 June 1985, a Boeing 747 operating on the route was blown up by a bomb mid-air off the coast of Ireland. A total of 329 people aboard were killed, 268 Canadian citizens, 27 British citizens and 24 Indian citizens, including the flight crew. On the same day, an explosion due to a luggage bomb was linked to the terrorist operation and occurred at the Narita Airport in Tokyo, Japan, intended for Air India Flight 301, killing two baggage handlers. The entire event was inter-continental in scope, killing 331 people in total and affected five countries on different continents: Canada, the United Kingdom, India, Japan, and Ireland.

The main suspects in the bombing were members of a Sikh separatist group called the Babbar Khalsa, and other related groups who were at the time agitating for a separate Sikh state of Khalistan in Punjab, India. In September 2007, the Canadian Commission of Inquiry investigated reports, initially disclosed in the Indian investigative news magazine Tehelka,that a hitherto unnamed person, Lakhbir Singh Rode, had masterminded the explosions. However, in conclusion two separate Canadian inquiries officially determined that the mastermind behind the terrorist operation was in fact the Canadian, Talwinder Singh Parmar.

Several men were arrested and tried for the Air India bombing. Inderjit Singh Reyat, a Canadian national and member of the International Sikh Youth Federation who pleaded guilty in 2003 to manslaughter, would be the only person convicted in the case. He was sentenced to fifteen years in prison for assembling the bombs that exploded on board Air India Flight 182 and at Narita Airport.

* Late 1980s

In 1986, when the insurgency was at its peak, the Golden Temple was again occupied by militants belonging to the All India Sikh Students Federation and Damdami Taksal. The militants called an assembly (Sarbat Khalsa) and, on 26 January, they would pass a resolution (gurmattā) in favour of the creation of Khalistan. However, only the Shiromani Gurdwara Parbandhak Committee (SGPC) had the authority to appoint the jathedar, the supreme religio-temporal seat of the Sikhs. The militants thus dissolved the SGPC and appointed their own jathedar, who turned out to refuse their bidding as well. Militant leader Gurbachan Singh Manochahal thereby appointed himself by force.

On 29 April 1986, an assembly of separatist Sikhs at the Akal Takht made a declaration of an independent state of Khalistan, and a number of rebel militant groups in favour of Khalistan subsequently waged a major insurgency against the Government of India. A decade of violence and conflict in Punjab would follow before a return to normality in the region. This period of insurgency saw clashes of Sikh militants with the police, as well as with the Nirankaris, a mystical Sikh sect who are less conservative in their aims to reform Sikhism.

The Khalistani militant activities manifested in the form of several attacks, such as the 1987 massacre of 32 Hindu bus passengers near Lalru, and the 1991 killing of 80 train passengers in Ludhiana.Such activities continued on into the 1990s as the perpetrators of the 1984 riots remained unpunished, while many Sikhs also felt that they were being discriminated against and that their religious rights were being suppressed.

In the parliamentary elections of 1989, Sikh separatist representatives were victorious in 10 of Punjab's 13 national seats and had the most popular support. The Congress cancelled those elections and instead hosted a Khaki election. The separatists boycotted the poll. The voter turnout was 24%. The Congress won this election and used it to further its anti-separatist campaign. Most of the separatist leadership was wiped out and the moderates were suppressed by end of 1993.

- 1990s

Indian security forces suppressed the insurgency in the early 1990s, while Sikh political groups such as the Khalsa Raj Party and SAD (A) continued to pursue an independent Khalistan through non-violent means. GlobalSecurity.org reported that in the early 1990s, journalists who did not conform to militant-approved behaviour were targeted for death.

It also reported that there were indiscriminate attacks designed to cause extensive civilian casualties: derailing trains, and exploding bombs in markets, restaurants, and other civilian areas between Delhi and Punjab. It further reported that militants assassinated many of those moderate Sikh leaders who opposed them, and sometimes killed rivals within the same militant group. It also stated that many civilians who had been kidnapped by extremists were murdered if the militants' demands were not met. Finally, it reported that Hindus left Punjab by the thousands. Whereas to take iron from the terrorists in the village Bhikhiwind, district Tarn Taran 'Sandhu' family fought everyday like the last day and defeated terrorists several times. One such incident was on 30 September 1990, when about 200 terrorists attacked Balwinder Singh's house. In retaliation, the Sandhu family using weapons provided by state police killed several and compiled the rest of the terrorists to run away. The Family awarded the Shaurya Chakra to show most conspicuous bravery, indomitable courage.

In August 1991, Julio Ribeiro, then-Indian Ambassador to Romania, was attacked and wounded at Bucharest in an assassination attempt by gunmen identified as Punjabi Sikhs.[88][80] Sikh groups also claimed responsibility for the 1991 kidnapping of Liviu Radu, the Romanian chargé d'affaires in New Delhi. This appeared to be in retaliation for Romanian arrests of Khalistan Liberation Force members suspected of the attempted assassination of Ribeiro. Radu was released unharmed after Sikh politicians criticised the action.

In October 1991, the New York Times reported that violence had increased sharply in the months leading up to the kidnapping, with Indian security forces or Sikh militants killing 20 or more people per day, and that the militants had been "gunning down" family members of police officers.[80] Scholar Ian Talbot states that all sides, including the Indian Army, police and the militants, committed crimes like murder, rape and torture.

From 24 January 1993 to 4 August 1993, Khalistan was a member of the NGO Unrepresented Nations and Peoples Organization. The membership was permanently suspended on 22 January 1995.

On 31 August 1995, Chief Minister Beant Singh was killed in a suicide bombing, for which the pro-Khalistan group Babbar Khalsa claimed responsibility. Security authorities, however, reported the group's involvement to be doubtful. A 2006 press release by the Embassy of the

United States in New Delhi indicated that the responsible organisation was the Khalistan Commando Force.

While the militants enjoyed some support among Sikh separatists in the earlier period, this support gradually disappeared.The insurgency weakened the Punjab economy and led to an increase in violence in the state. With dwindling support and increasingly-effective Indian security troops eliminating anti-state combatants, Sikh militancy effectively ended by the early 1990s.

- 2000s Retribution

There have been serious charges levelled by human rights activists against Indian Security forces (headed by Sikh police officer, K. P. S. Gill), claiming that thousands of suspects were killed in staged shootouts and thousands of bodies were cremated/disposed of without proper identification or post-mortems. Human Rights Watch reported that, since 1984, government forces had resorted to widespread human rights violations to fight the militants, including: arbitrary arrest, prolonged detention without trial, torture, and summary executions of civilians and suspected militants. Family members were frequently detained and tortured to reveal the whereabouts of relatives sought by the police. Amnesty International has alleged several cases of disappearances, torture, rape, and unlawful detentions by the police during the Punjab insurgency, for which 75–100 police officers had been convicted by December 2002.

- Present-day activities

Present-day activities by Khalistani militants include the Tarn Taran blast, in which a police crackdown arrested 4 terrorists, one of whom revealed they were ordered by Sikhs for Justice to kill multiple Dera leaders in India. Pro-Khalistan organisations such as Dal Khalsa are also active outside India, supported by a section of the Sikh diaspora. As of 25 December, there also have been inputs by multiple agencies about a possible attack in Punjab by Babbar Khalsa and Khalistan Zindabad Force, according to Indian Media sources, are allegedly in contact with their Pakistani handlers and are trying to smuggle arms across the border.

In November 2015, a congregation of the Sikh community (i.e. a Sarbat Khalsa) was called in response to recent unrest in the Punjab region. The

Sarbat Khalsa adopted 13 resolutions to strengthen Sikh institutions and traditions. The 12th resolution reaffirmed the resolutions adopted by the Sarbat Khalsa in 1986, including the declaration of the sovereign state of Khalistan.

Moreover, signs in favour of Khalistan were raised when SAD (Amritsar) President Simranjeet Singh Mann met with Surat Singh Khalsa, who was admitted to Dayanand Medical College & Hospital (DMCH). While Mann was arguing with ACP Satish Malhotra, supporters standing at the main gate of DMCH raised Khalistan signs in the presence of heavy police force. After a confrontation with the police authorities that lasted about 15–20 minutes, Mann was allowed to meet Khalsa along with ADCP Paramjeet Singh Pannu.

Despite residing outside India, there is a strong sense of attachment among Sikhs to their culture and religion. As such, Sikh groups operating from other countries could potentially revive the Khalistan Movement. There is persistent demand for justice for the Sikh victims during the peak of the Khalistan movement. In some ways, The Sikh diaspora can be seen as torch-bearers of the Khalistan movement, which is now considered to be highly political and military in nature. Recent reports indicate a rise in pro-Khalistan sentiments among the Sikh diaspora overseas who can revive the secessionist movement. Some people were even spotted during the World Cup 2019 in pro-khalistan jerseys, but were then whisked out of the stadium.

- Recently, many signs have been raised in several places in support of the Khalistan movement, although the Immigration and Refugee Board of Canada (IRCC) reports that Sikhs who support Khalistan may themselves be detained and tortured. Notably, on the 31st anniversary of Operation Bluestar, pro-Khalistan signs were raised in Punjab, resulting in 25 Sikh youths being detained by police. Pro-Khalistan signs were also raised during a function of Punjabi Chief Minister Parkash Singh Badal. Two members of SAD-A, identified as Sarup Singh Sandha and Rajindr Singh Channa, raised pro-Khalistan and anti-Badal signs during the chief minister's speech.

In retrospect, the Khalistan movement has failed to reach its objectives in India due to several reasons:

Heavy Police crackdown on the separatists under the leadership of Punjab Police chief KPS Gill. Several militant leaders were killed and others surrendered and rehabilitated.

Gill credits the decline to change in the policies by adding provision for an adequate number of police and security forces to deal with the militancy. The clear political will from the government without any interference.

Lack of a clear political concept of 'Khalistan' even to the extremist supporters. As per Kumar (1997), the name which was wishful thinking only represented their revulsion against the Indian establishment and did not find any alternative to it.

1. In the later stages of the movement, militants lacked an ideological motivation.
2. The entry of criminals and government loyalists into its ranks further divided the groups.
3. Loss of sympathy and support from the Sikh population of Punjab.

The divisions among the Sikhs also undermined this movement. According to Pettigrew non-Jat urban Sikhs did not want to live in a country of "Jatistan." Further division was caused as the people in the region traditionally preferred police and military service as career options. The Punjab Police had a majority of Jat Sikhs and the conflict was referred as "Jat against Jat" by Police Chief Gill.

- Militancy

During the late 1980s and the early 1990s, there was a dramatic rise in radical State militancy in Punjab. The 1984 military Operation Blue Star in the Golden Temple in Amritsar offended many Sikhs. The separatists used this event, as well as the following Anti-Sikh Riots, to claim that the interest of Sikhs was not safe in India and to foster the spread of militancy among Sikhs in Punjab. Some sections of the Sikh diaspora also began join the separatists with financial and diplomatic support.

A section of Sikhs turned to militancy in Punjab and several Sikh militant outfits proliferated in the 1980s and 1990s.Some militant groups aimed to create an independent state through acts of violence directed at members of the Indian government, army, or forces. A large numbers of Sikhs condemned the actions of the militants. According to anthropological analysis, one reason young men had for joining militant and other religious nationalist groups was for fun, excitement, and expressions of masculinity.

Puri, Judge, and Sekhon (1999) suggest that illiterate/under-educated young men, lacking enough job prospects, had joined pro-Khalistan militant groups for the primary purpose of "fun." They mention that the pursuit of Khalistan itself was the motivation for only 5% of "militants."

* Khalistani groups

There are several militant Sikh groups, such as the Khalistan Council, that are currently functional and provides organization and guidance to the Sikh community. Multiple groups are organized across the world, coordinating their military efforts for Khalistan. Such groups were most active in 1980s and early 1990s, and have since receded in activity. These groups are largely defunct in India but they still have a political presence among the Sikh diaspora, especially in countries such as Pakistan where they are not prescribed by law.

Most of these outfits were crushed by 1993 during the counter-insurgency operations. In recent years, active groups have included Babbar Khalsa, International Sikh Youth Federation, Dal Khalsa, and Bhindranwale Tiger Force. An unknown group before then, the Shaheed Khalsa Force claimed credit for the marketplace bombings in New Delhi in 1997. The group has never been heard of since.

* *Shaheed Khalsa Force*

* Abatement

The U.S. Department of State found that Sikh extremism had decreased significantly from 1992 to 1997, although a 1997 report noted that "Sikh militant cells are active internationally and extremists gather funds from overseas Sikh communities."

In 1999, Kuldip Nayar, writing for Rediff.com, stated in an article, titled "It is fundamentalism again", that the Sikh "masses" had rejected terrorists. By 2001, Sikh extremism and the demand for Khalistan had all but abated.

Reported in his paper, titled "From Bhindranwale to Bin Laden: Understanding Religious Violence", Director Mark Juergensmeyer of the Orfalea Centre for Global & International Studies, UCSB, interviewed a militant who said that "the movement is over," as many of his colleagues had been killed, imprisoned, or driven into hiding, and because public support was gone.

- Outside of India

Operation Blue Star and its violent aftermaths popularized the demand for Khalistan among many Sikhs dispersed globally.Involvement of sections of Sikh diaspora turned out to be important for the movement as it provided the diplomatic and financial support. It also enabled Pakistan to become involved in the fueling of the movement. Sikhs in UK, Canada and USA arranged for cadres to travel to Pakistan for military and financial assistance. Some Sikh groups abroad even declared themselves as the Khalistani government in exile.

The Sikh place of worship, gurdwaras provided the geographic and institutional coordination for the Sikh community. Sikh political factions have used the gurdwaras as a forum for political organization. The gurdwaras sometimes served as the site for mobilization of diaspora for Khalistan movement directly by raising funds. Indirect mobilization was sometimes provided by promoting a stylized version of conflict and Sikh history. The rooms in some gurdwara exhibit pictures of Khalistani leaders along with paintings of martyrs from Sikh history. Gurdwaras also host speakers and musical groups that promote and encourage the movement. Among the diasporas, Khalistan issue has been a divisive issue within gurdwaras. These factions have fought over the control of gurdwaras and their political and financial resources. The fights between pro and anti-Khalistan factions over gurdwaras often included violent acts and bloodshed as reported from UK and North America. The gurdwaras with Khalistani leadership allegedly funnel the collected funds into activities supporting the movement.

Different groups of Sikhs in the diaspora organize the convention of international meetings to facilitate communication and establish organizational order. In April 1981 the first "International Convention of Sikhs," was held in New York and was attended by some 200 delegates. In April 1987 the third convention was held in Slough, Berkshire where the Khalistan issue was addressed. This meeting's objective was to "build unity in the Khalistan movement."

All these factors further strengthened the emerging nationalism among Sikhs. Sikh organizations launched many fund-raising efforts that were used for several purposes. After 1984 one of the objectives was the promotion of the Sikh version of "ethnonational history" and the relationship with the Indian state. The Sikh diaspora also increased their efforts to build institutions to maintain and propagate their ethnonational heritage. A major objective of these educational efforts was to publicize a different face to the non Sikh international community who regarded the Sikhs as "terrorists."

In 1993, Khalistan was briefly admitted in the Unrepresented Nations and Peoples Organization, but was suspended in a few months. The membership suspension was made permanent on 22 January 1995.

* Pakistan

Pakistan has long aspired to dismember India through its Bleed India strategy. Even before the Indo-Pakistani War of 1971, Zulfikar Ali Bhutto, then a member of the military regime of General Yahya Khan, stated, "Once the back of Indian forces is broken in the east, Pakistan should occupy the whole of Eastern India and make it a permanent part of East Pakistan.... Kashmir should be taken at any price, even the Sikh Punjab and turned into Khalistan."

General Zia-ul Haq, who succeeded Bhutto as the Head of State, attempted to reverse the traditional antipathy between Sikhs and Muslims arising from the partition violence by restoring Sikh shrines in Pakistan and opening them for Sikh pilgrimage. The expatriate Sikhs from England and North America that visited these shrines were at the forefront of the calls for Khalistan. During the pilgrims' stay in Pakistan, the Sikhs were exposed to Khalistani propaganda, which would not be openly possible in India.[The ISI chief, General Abdul Rahman, opened a cell within ISI with the objective of supporting the "[Sikhs']...freedom struggle against India". Rahman's colleagues in ISI took pride in the fact that "the Sikhs were able to set the whole province on fire. They knew who to kill, where to plant a bomb and which office to target." General Hamid Gul argued that keeping Punjab destabilized was equivalent to the Pakistan Army having an extra division at no cost. Zia-ul Haq, on the other hand, consistently practised the art of plausible denial. The Khalistan movement was brought to a decline only after India fenced off a part of the Punjab border with Pakistan and the Benazir Bhutto government agreed to joint patrols of the border by Indian and Pakistani troops.

In 2006, an American Court convicted Khalid Awan, a Muslim and Canadian of Pakistani descent, of "supporting terrorism" by providing money and financial services to the Khalistan Commando Force chief Paramjit Singh Panjwar in Pakistan. KCF members had carried out deadly attacks against Indian civilians causing thousands of deaths. Awan frequently travelled to Pakistan and was alleged by the U.S. officials with links to Sikh and Muslim extremists, as well as Pakistani intelligence.

In 2008, India's Intelligence Bureau indicated that Pakistan's Inter-Services Intelligence organisation was trying to revive Sikh militancy.

Indian Airlines Flight 423

- Indian Airlines Flight 423

Indian Airlines Flight 423 (IATA No.: IC423) was an Indian Airlines Boeing 737 domestic passenger flight from the Delhi-Palam Airport to the Amritsar-Raja Sansi Airport on 29 September 1981. It was hijacked by five Sikh militants of the Dal Khalsa (armed with daggers and a hand grenade), masterminded by Sikh militants and taken to Lahore Airport in Pakistan. The plane had 111 passengers and 6 crew members on board. The Dal Khalsa had been demanding a separate Sikh homeland of Khalistan.

The leader of the hijackers, Gajender Singh, talked to Natwar Singh, India's ambassador in Pakistan, and put forward his demands. Singh had demanded the release of his leaders, including Jarnail Singh Bhindranwale, and a sum of $500,000 in cash.

Pakistan agreed to India's request to ensure the passenger's safety in spite of protests by Pakistani intelligence agency ISI. Pakistan took commando action using its elite SSG which cleared the plane and got all passengers released. The hijackers faced trial in Pakistan and they were sentenced to life imprisonment.

The accused, Satnam Singh, after completing his trial, returned to India and was put on retrial. However the court discharged him, stating that the accused has already served the sentence in Pakistan.

CHAPTER TWO

List of hijackings of Indian aeroplanes

- List of hijackings of Indian aeroplanes

1970s

1971 January 30 : An Indian Airlines plane on its way from Srinagar to Jammu was hijacked by Hashim Quereshi and Ashraf Quereshi of the JKLF, who took it to Lahore. Zulfikar Ali Bhutto, then Foreign Minister of Pakistan rushed to Lahore and met the hijacker. On February 1, he persuaded them to release the crew and passengers who were then sent by road to Amritsar. The Government of India sought permission of Pakistan to send a replacement crew to fly the aircraft back to India. Pakistan authorities denied the permission, and the hijackers torched the aircraft on February 2.

1976 September 10: Indian Airlines plane Boeing 737 was hijacked from Palam Airport Delhi by a group of six terrorists from Kashmir: Syed Abdul Hameed Dewani along, Syed M Rafique, M Ahsan Rathore, Abdul Rashid Malik, Ghulam Rasool and Khawaja Ghulam Nabi Itoo. Initially ordered to fly the plane to Libya, after knowing that there wasn't enough fuel for that journey , the leader of the terrorists told the pilot Captain B.N Reddy to take the flight to Karachi, Pakistan instead.

To refuel the plane, they took permission from CAA Lahore airport in Pakistan to land and refuel. All the passengers and crew on board were duly returned to India the next day, after diplomatic relations between India and Pakistan were re-established and Pakistan helped with the rescue operations.The hijackers were caught in a trick during breakfast, being served colourless tranquilliser with water. All six hijackers were taken in custody and the plane was sent back to India with 83 passengers on board. The militants were later released in Pakistan citing "lack of evidence". Repercussions on the Indian side led to the suspension of 11 members of the security staff and a promise by the Minister for Tourism and Civil Aviation, Raj Bahadur, to order a detailed and "thorough inquiry" into the event "and into the security arrangements at the airport".

1978 December 20: Indian Airlines flight 410 was hijacked mid-air minutes before it's touchdown at the erstwhile Palam Airport, New Delhi. The two terrorists, Bholanath Pandey and Devendra Pandey, who were both rumoured to be members of Youth Congress hijacked the Indian Airlines plane on a domestic flight from Calcutta to Delhi. They demanded the release of opposition leader Indira Gandhi (who had been arrested by Indian parliament) and the withdrawal of all the cases against her son Sanjay Gandhi. They also demanded that the Janata party government at the centre give their resignation and leave. Initially the two demanded to fly the plane to Nepal and then Bangladesh, both of which were rejected due to shortage of fuel. Eventually the flight was taken to Varanasi where the flight was landed. It was here that the chief minister of the state of Uttar Pradesh was summoned for the negotiations. After much debacle and discussions both men released the passengers and crew. Their surrender in the presence of media was noted.In the aftermath of this hijacking the Congress party was criticised as a fascist regime. Jarnail Singh Bhindrawale also used this as a point to criticize the hypocrisy of the Indian government even though the government has repeatedly denied its involvement and thus any blame.

* *1980s*

1981 September 29: An Indian Airlines IC-423 plane on flight from Delhi to Amritsar was hijacked by Sikh separatists and taken to Lahore. Pakistan took commando action using its elite SSG, which cleared the plane and freed all passengers.

1981 November 25: Air India Flight 224, a Boeing 707 plane VT-DVB "Kamet" on its way from Zambia to Mumbai, with 65 passengers and 13 crew members, was hijacked when it landed for refuelling at Mahe, Seychelles.The 43-strong team of mercenaries carrying an assortment of weapons demanded that the flight to be taken to Durban where the nightmare of the crew and the passengers ended after prolonged negotiations.

1982 August 4: An Indian Airlines flight from Delhi-Srinagar was hijacked en-route by a Sikh militant with the help of a fake bomb. The hijacker identified as Gurbaksh Singh hijacked the plane, by his own statement as direct retaliation after the Indian government has then asked Sikhs to not carry their Kirpans(Sikh ceremonial daggers) onboard. The hijacked plane landed at Amritsar (after being denied permission to land in Lahore, Pakistan. After landing in Amritsar he demanded that he would list his demands only in the presence of then Shiromani Akali Dal president Harchand Singh Longowal and then Damdami Taksal chief Jarnail Singh Bhindranwale, but he later surrendered in front of then SAD general secretary Parkash Singh Majitha. All the crew and passengers on board which included 70 foreigners were rescued successfully.

1982 August 20: A Sikh militant, armed with a pistol and a hand grenade, hijacked a Boeing 737 on a scheduled flight from Jodhpur to New Delhi carrying 69 persons. The militant got on the plane at Udaipur on the jump flight from Bombay to Delhi stopping at Jodhpur, Udaipur and Jaipur. The hijacker was later identified as Manjit Singh an electrician from Amritsar. The militant demanded for the flight to be taken to Lahore but after being debited permission to land by the Pakistani government, it was no longer possible. Due to this the plane circled over Lahore airport more than 42 times before running short of fuel, due to which it was finally landed at Amritsar.

- Among the various demands that Manjit asked for was 8 Lakh Rupees in German marks, the transfer of power in Punjab to Akali Dal with the position of chief minister given to Prakash Singh Badal and the release of half Sikh security granthis. The hijacker was finally apprehended and shot dead in what was described in a rather "Ham handed" manner. All the passengers and crew on the plane were successfully rescued by the Punjab police and commandos. Peter Lamont, production designer working on the James Bond film Octopussy, was a passenger.

1984 July 5 : An Indian Airlines jet IC 405 carrying 254 passengers and a crew of ten on flight from Srinagar to New Delhi was hijacked and forced to land in Lahore, Pakistan. The hijackers were reported to be armed with pistols, daggers and explosives. The hijackers' surrender to Pakistani authorities ended a 17-hour ordeal for the plane's passengers and crew, who remained aboard the A-300 Airbus in suffocating heat, with little food and water.

1984 August 24: Seven young hijackers demanded an Indian Airlines jetliner IC 421, on a domestic flight from Delhi to Srinagar with 100 passengers on board, be flown to the United States. The plane was taken to Lahore, Karachi and finally to Dubai where the defense minister of UAE negotiated the release of the passengers. It was related to the secessionist struggle in the Indian state of Punjab. The hijacker was subsequently extradited by UAE authorities to India, who handed over the pistol recovered from the hijacker.

1986 September 5: Boeing 747-121 serving the flight from Bombay, India, to New York, United States with 360 passengers on board, was hijacked while on the ground at Karachi by four armed Palestinian men of the Abu Nidal Organization. Forty-three passengers were injured or killed during the hijacking, including nationals from India, the United States, Pakistan, and Mexico. All the hijackers were arrested and sentenced to death in Pakistan; however, 4 of the hijackers remain at large. The 2016 Bollywood movie Neerja is based on this event, with focus on the actions of flight purser Neerja Bhanot.

• 1990s

1993 January 22: Indian Airlines Flight 810 en route from Lucknow Airport to the Delhi-Indira Gandhi International Airport was hijacked and returned to Lucknow. The hijacker demanded the release of all karsevaks arrested after the Demolition of the Babri Masjid situated in Ayodhya and for a temple be built at Ram Janmabhoomi which according to extremists was situated at the site of the mosque. The hijacker later identified as Satish Chandra Pandey stated his reason for the hijacking, as a means of protest for them Prime minister Narasimha Rao's assurance that Babri Masjid would be remade. The hijacker surrendered after talking to then MP from Lucknow Atal Bihari Vajpayee, former prime minister of India. The bomb he carried was also found to be phony.

1993 March 27: Indian Airlines Flight 439 was hijacked en route from Delhi to Madras by a hijacker claiming to be strapped with explosives. The hijacker was later identified as Hari Singh, a truck driver from Haryana. He stated the reason behind this hijacking as a protest against the ongoing Hindu-Muslim riots at that time in which more than 2,000 people lost their lives.He forced the plane to land in Amritsar (after being denied landing permission in Lahore) and demanded political asylum in Pakistan. His demands of a 40 day asylum in Pakistan and permission to speak to Pakistani media was rejected but, was allowed to speak to Indian media at Amritsar airport after his surrender. The hijacker subsequently surrendered and the explosive was found to be a disguised hair-dryer.

1993 April 10: An Indian Airlines Boeing 737-2A8, en route from Lucknow to Delhi, was hijacked by four students of the Government Arts College, Lucknow. The 4 youth commandeered the plane soon after takeoff from Lucknow and forced it return. The 4 students were armed with a bottle which they brandished as containing an explosive. It was later identified as being a combustible liquid capable of a small fire. They demanded changes to the college's courses, cancellation of an award to a professor and postponement of exams. One student narrated a 10 minute litany on their various grievances and demanded that unless they are allowed to meet with the governor of Uttar Pradesh they'll blow up the plane. In the words Tom Segev, an Israeli Journalist who was also a passenger on the flight "The whole thing was like a game."

- The passengers didn't put much attention to the hijackers and continued to do whatever they were doing. The flight flew in circles for 3 hours, while negotiations were done with the authorities through the control tower. After the flight landed the passengers overpowered the hijackers and successfully got the situation in control. All of the 52 passengers and 7 crew members were unharmed and saved. The hijackers beaten and bruised were handed over to authorities. This was the 3rd attempt on plane hijacking in 1993.

1993 April 24: Indian Airlines aircraft bound for Srinagar via Jammu from Delhi is hijacked. The hijacker wanted to take the plane to Lahore, but Pakistan authorities refused permission. The plane landed at Amritsar where the hijacker was killed and passengers freed.

1999-2000: Indian Airlines Flight 814, flying from Kathmandu, is hijacked and diverted to Kandahar. After a week-long stand-off, India agrees to release three jailed terrorists in exchange for the hostages. One hostage was stabbed to death and his body thrown on the tarmac as a "warning attack".

CHAPTER THREE

Bell Bottom (2021 film)

- Bell Bottom (2021 film)

1. During writing this book no character & no religious are harmed written by Mr Vivek Kumar Pandey. winner youngest writer award 1ˢᵗ rank in india 2020.He is only one writer can publish 700+ own book that was greatest successfull in his life
2. In This Book Deeply Given About Hijacking Of Indian Aeroplane.Totally Bell Bottom Film Based On This Real Story Of Hijacking Of Planes.

Bell Bottom is a 2021 Indian Hindi-language action thriller filmdirected by Ranjit M Tewari. The film is written by Aseem Arrora and Parveez Sheikh, with production by Vashu Bhagnani, Jackky Bhagnani, Deepshikha Deshmukh and Nikkhil Advani under their respective banners Pooja Entertainment and Emmay Entertainment. It stars Akshay Kumar as the lead character, with Lara Dutta, Vaani Kapoor and Huma Qureshi in an extended cameo appearance. Bell Bottom is inspired from real life hijacking events in India by Khalistani separatists during the 1980s, such as the Indian Airlines Flight 423, 405 and 421 hijackings.

Principal photography began on 20 August 2020. The film was wrapped up on 30 September in London. The film released in theatres on 19 August 2021 in 3D. The film received mixed to positive reviews, praising Kumar's and Dutta's performance, art direction, fast paced narration & screenplay, background music & cinematography, but criticised the low quality VFX shots in action sequences and weak climax.

- Plot

In 1984, Indian Airlines Flight 691 (resembling Indian Airlines Flight 421) is hijacked, the seventh such hijacking in India in five years, with all the previous ones ending in acquiescence to the hijackers' demands that other terrorists be freed and money be delivered. During her briefing, Prime Minister Indira Gandhi, frustrated at the lack of action taken on the matter, decides to allow a RAW agent code-named "Bell Bottom" to handle the case. As a "mere" clerk, he is already viewed with consternation by the other officials, and his deduction that the alleged masterminds, a Khalistan separatist group named "Azaadi Dal" (lit. 'Liberation Organisation'), are merely a front for Pakistan's ISI are rebuffed by them due to improving Indo-Pakistani relations. After the plane lands in Amritsar when he predicted it would land in Lahore, he is dismissed. However, his supervisor points out that he is an expert on hijackings and is motivated by personal experience.

In 1979, polymath Anshul Malhotra lives with his mother Raavi, an asthmatic who constantly visits his brother in London, and his wife Radhika. Her flight is hijacked by terrorists, but then-PM Morarji Desai and Pakistani President Muhammad Zia-ul-Haq negotiate and fulfill the hijackers demands in exchange for the hostages' release. However, Raavi dies, reportedly due to natural causes. Soon after, though, Anshul is abducted by RAW, who reveal that one of the hijackers, Daljeet "Doddy" Singh, had purposely withheld her inhaler, pusher her into the galley and thrown heavy blankets on her, increasing her suffering as she died. Anshul is given the offer to join RAW; he accepts and takes on the code-name Bell Bottom, with his cover to his wife being that he is an embassy officer. After his training, which showcases his extraordinary memory and improves his previously subpar physical skills, he is assigned to the hijacking desk. In 1983, he finds one of the hijackers while visiting his brother in London and tracks them; he raids their house with other RAW agents and captures three of them but the fourth, Doddy Singh, escapes.

Back in the present, the plane takes off from Amritsar and lands in Lahore, prompting Gandhi to order Anshul back in. He convinces her to "break script" and disallow the Pakistani side to send their negotiating team, and orders them not to refuel the plane. In response, Zia sends his minister to keep track of the situation. In Lahore, the minister replaces the hijacker with Doddy and supplies weapons and explosives. Correctly figuring that they will go to the Middle East to take advantage of their naivety in aerial terrorism, Anshul prepares for a covert operation in Dubai against the

Indian ministers' wishes. Meanwhile, the Pakistani minister goes to Dubai to observe what is going on and guide Doddy.

Upon arrival, Anshul and his team, disguised as diplomatic aides, meet up with a contact in the Dubai airport, where they see Dubai's emphasis on humanitarianism and avoidance of bloodshed. Their first plan, covertly entering the aircraft and disarming the hijackers, is foiled when the Pakistani minister notices and closes the luggage door. Anshul's "plan B", sending in the Indian army, is also curtailed when the Dubai officials are notified and the ship they are on is denied entry. With all avenues cut off, the ministers go to negiotate; although they agree to the terrorists' demands of money, more terrorist releases, and a charter flight to London for freedom, they are surprised at the terrorists extreme inhumanity and one of them is taken hostage as a "VIP" target to be held until they get to London. Seemingly out of options, Anshul asks their airport contact to take them to a under-construction terminal so they can view the proceedings; however this is a ruse as Anshul reveals his knowledge of the contact's betrayal and ties her up.

Disguising themselves as airport workers, they take advantage of a sandstorm to get on the field, free the VIPs, and capture the terrorists, redirecting the charter flight to India. The leader of Dubai denies them take off clearance at first, but after Anshul explains how their methods fit in with Dubai's humanism, he grants it. In India, the terrorists are booked, with Zia and the ISI leaders huffing in disgrace, and the flight is returned, with all on board safe and sound and reunited with their families. In the end, it is revealed that Radhika was actually working for RAW and had informed them of her husband's abilities and background in the first place.

1. Cast
2. Akshay Kumar as Anshul Malhotra / Agent Bell Bottom
3. Lara Dutta as Prime Minister Indira Gandhi
4. Vaani Kapoor as Radhika Malhotra
5. Huma Qureshi as Adeela Rehman
6. Adil Hussain as N. F. Suntook
7. Denzil Smith as R. N. Kao
8. Aniruddh Dave as Puchchi
9. Thalaivasal Vijay as P. V. Narasimha Rao
10. Zain Khan Durrani as Daljeet Singh aka Doddy
11. Dolly Ahluwalia as Raavie Malhotra

12. Mamik Singh as Aashu Malhotra
13. Abhijit Lahiri as Khurshed Alam Khan
14. Sumit Kaul as Dollar
15. Sunit Tandon as ISI Chief
16. Jatin Negi as Sundar
17. Amit Kumar Vashisth as Saand
18. Kavi Raj as Gen. Muhammad Zia-ul-Haq
19. Husam Chadat as Farhad Bin Sultan
20. Anjali Dinesh Anand as Anshul's Sister-In-Law
21. Ashok Chhabra as Morarji Desai
22. Balram Gupta as Home Minister
23. Girish Sharma as Anshul's Friend
24. Nitin Khanna as Dubai Policeman
25. Karim Saidi as Abu Mukhtar
26. Deesh Mariwala as Tejeshwar
27. Ahmed Yahya Berrada as IB Official Of Dubai

- Production and release

The film was officially announced in November 2019 with release date of Republic Day 2021. Bell Bottom is based on true events and the story is set during the 1980s about some unforgettable heroes of the era. It is Vaani Kapoor's first film to be not produced by Yash Raj Films and became the first Bollywood movie to start shooting amid the COVID-19 pandemic in 2020 during which shootings were stopped in India.The film's theatrical premiere was postponed to 2 April 2021 in January 2020. The cast and crew of the film flew to Glasgow, Scotland in the first week of August 2020. The filming eventually kicked off on 20 August 2020.The film was wrapped up on 30 September in London. The film's release was postponed due to the second wave of the COVID-19 pandemic throughout India. The film finally released theatrically on 19 August 2021 in 3D.

- LabelSaregama Music

The film score is composed by Daniel B. George while Julius Packiam composed the trailer score. The songs featured in the film are composed by Amaal Mallik, Tanishk Bagchi, Shantanu Dutta, Gurnazar and Maninder Buttar while lyrics are written by Rashmi Virag, Tanishk Bagchi, Babbu

Maan, Maninder Buttar, Seema Saini and Gurnazar.

- thank you for buy & read this book

  have a great day of your
  from : Mr Vivek Kumar Pandey

- This All Credit Goes To My Super Hero Daddy. Always Love You dad